FLYING BOAT
H

JOHN EVANS

John Evans.

The official badge of RAF Pembroke Dock showing a Manx Shearwater on one of the islands off Pembrokeshire's western coast. The Welsh motto means 'Watching the West from the Air', succinctly reflecting Pembroke Dock's unique role as aerial guardian of the Western Approaches to Britain.

MINISTRY OF DEFENCE

On 31st March, 1930, the former Royal Dockyard was transferred from the Admiralty to the Air Ministry, ushering in Pembroke Dock's all too brief air era.

Exactly 29 years later - on 31st March, 1959 - the RAF Standard was ceremonially lowered for the last time in the air station, bringing to a close a remarkable chapter in the history of this military town.

There was to be a short postscript when a Sunderland - the most famous of all the flying-boats - returned to Pembroke Dock in March, 1961, for preservation. Ten years later this same Sunderland, ML824, left Pembroke Dock for the RAF Museum at Hendon, and a major link with the past was severed, sadly for ever.

In the three decades starting in 1930 the town of Pembroke Dock and its RAF station were perfect partners. Begun as a Dockyard town, Pembroke Dock had good reason to respect its Air Force residents and the townspeople celebrated the good times and mourned the sad times along with the RAF.

Known simply as 'PD' throughout the RAF, Pembroke Dock was a happy and popular station, and its flying-boat days covered some of the most turbulent years of this century. There were several phases:

* The early years when the RAF worked effectively to establish Pembroke Dock as a major air station.
* The expansion period from the mid-1930's onwards when RAF Pembroke Dock grew in stature as war clouds loomed over Europe.
* The long hard years of the Second World War; six years in the forefront of the bitterest war in history.
* The post-war era when flying-boats still graced the sky and the water, making an unique contribution to the peacetime role of the RAF.
* And, almost as an afterthought, the preservation of Sunderland ML824 and its display at Pembroke Dock for 10 years.

This book is not a history of RAF Pembroke Dock but represents a collection of photographs reflecting something of the periods of history of this remarkable town and its air station.

Originally published in 1985 at the time of the First Pembroke Dock Flying-Boat Reunion, it has been reprinted several times.

The photographs come from the collection of aviation historian John Evans. Pembrokeshire-born, he resides in Pembroke Dock and is researching the history of the RAF station once located in his home town. His principal aviation interests are in flying-boats and the maritime air war and in the history of the Royal Air Force and Fleet Air Arm in general.

John Evans is the originator of the idea to stage Flying-Boat Reunions in Pembroke Dock and is the Honorary Administrator of the all-voluntary Reunion organisation which maintains regular contacts with around 2,000 people worldwide, all of whom have some connection with flying-boats.

He can be contacted at 6 Laws Street, Pembroke Dock, SA72 6DL, Tel: 01646 683041

ACKNOWLEDGEMENT is made to the many people who have generously loaned photographs for use in this book and who have greatly helped with my researches into 'PD' and flying-boat history. My thanks also to the staff of CIT Printing Services, Merlins Bridge, Haverfordwest, for their expertise and assistance once again, and to my research colleague and friend, Ted Goddard, for his editorial assistance and his help on various maritime questions.

JOHN EVANS
Pembroke Dock, March, 1998.

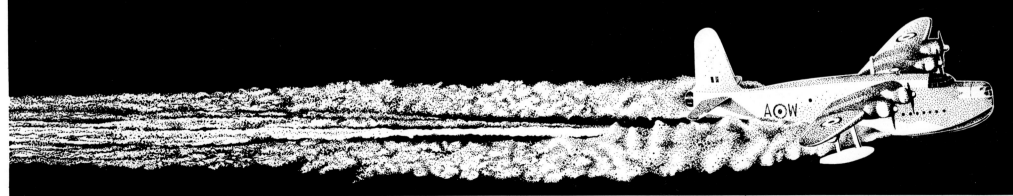

Naval visitor: Before the arrival of Pembroke Dock's first resident aircraft, the Haven Waterway had been used by flying boats and seaplanes of both the RAF and the Royal Navy. This photograph — dated 1930 — shows a Royal Navy Fairey IIIF floatplane, S1198, thought to be attached to the Second Cruiser Squadron. Royal Navy warships were regular visitors to the Haven in the 1930's and 111F floatplanes were used on Navy catapult flights.

CARSLEY COLLECTION

The full RAF Pembroke Dock line-up in 1932. Members of the RAF Police and Marine Craft Section join with officers and men of No. 210 Squadron and Station Headquarters. Wing Commander Bob Leckie, CO of No. 210 Squadron, is centre, front row, and with the RAF officers in the same row are Flight Lieutenant H. A. Castaldini (second from left) and Flight Lieutenant W. Liniker (second from right).

W. LINIKER

The first RAF officer at the Service's newest air station in 1930 was Flight Lieutenant Bill Liniker. His association with the station was a long one and he remained as the Equipment Officer at RAF Pembroke Dock until promoted to the Air Ministry in May 1939. Bill Liniker was the first Commanding Officer, relinquishing his command to Wing Commander Bob Leckie, CO of No. 210 Squadron, in 1931. Flight Lieutenant Liniker — who went on to become a Group Captain during the war — is pictured with the RAF Police contingent at Pembroke Dock in 1930. Front row (left to right): Jim Dooley, Flight Lieutenant W. Liniker, Sergeant Dick Johns; Back row (left to right): Jack Baskerville, Jack Perkins, Bert Greenaway, Charlie Morris, — Fitzpatrick.

W. LINIKER

Everyone smartly posing for the cameraman, but the dogs require disciplining! Wing Commander Bob Leckie, DSO, DSC, DFC, with one other officer and the NCOs of Station Headquarters c.1932. On Wing Commander Leckie's left is Warrant Officer II T. E. Charlesworth. Previously holding the old RAF rank of Sergeant Major, Warrant Officer Charlesworth later worked in a civilian capacity at the RAF base. Wing Commander Leckie left Pembroke Dock at the end of 1932 on promotion to Group Captain and became Superintendent of Reserve at RAF Hendon. He retired as an Air Marshal in 1947 and returned to live in Canada. At Pembroke Dock his successor was Wing Commander A. T. Harris, OBE, AFC, later to become the famous leader of Bomber Command during the Second World War.

MRS. A. M. TAYLOR

Lions roaring . . . Southampton S1231, its Napier Lions at full power, prepares to take off near the RAF station. S1231 was a Southampton Mark II with a metal hull.

K. EVANS

One of the first of many flying-boats to see service at RAF Pembroke Dock, a Supermarine Southampton, airborne over the Pembrokeshire coast. Apart from the Sunderland, Southamptons were the longest-serving RAF flying-boat, 68 of which were used between 1925 and 1936. The five-man crew consisted of a pilot and second pilot, in tandem open cockpits; a wireless operator/air gunner; a front gunner/bomb aimer and another gunner. Powered by two Napier Lion engines, the Southampton's maximum speed was 108 mph and the normal range was 770 miles. It could carry a 1,100 lb bomb load and defensive armament was three Lewis guns.

K. EVANS

▷ *RAF Pembroke Dock in its early days. This aerial view, presumably taken from a Southampton, shows the station as it looked in 1933, still with a very derelict air about it. The two large hangars still have to be built, but work is progressing on the slipway — an essential requirement for any flying-boat station. The first of the hangars was built in 1934.*

K. EVANS

"SOUTHAMPTON"

The men of the Seaplane Dock, 1932. Front row (l to r): Corporal Stephenson, Flight Lieutenant H. A. Castaldini, Sergeant Unknown. Back row (l to r): Unknown (the cook), 'Taff' Williamson, LAC Hedges, 'Taff' Vale, AC1 H. Rogers.

H. ROGERS

Routine Orders and New Orders stay pinned to the station notice board as 12 officers of No. 210 Squadron line up for an official photograph in 1932. Not all have been identified. With Wing Commander Bob Leckie (centre) are front row, fifth from left, Flight Lieutenant A. C. Stevens, later Air Marshal Sir Alick Stevens, Air Officer Commanding in Chief of Coastal Command, 1951-53; third from left, Squadron Leader A. F. Lang, later to become an Air Vice-Marshal, and, extreme left, Flying Officer R. L. Mills. In the back row are: fourth from left, Flying Officer Gordon, a New Zealander, centre, Flying Officer Biggs, and, first left, Pilot Officer D. C. T. Bennett, an Australian who later became Air Vice-Marshal Donald Bennett, the renowned leader of the Pathfinder Force in the Second World War. Flying Officer B. A. Frazer may be next to Donald Bennett. Officers on 210 Squadron at the beginning of 1932 are listed as: Wing Commander Leckie; Squadron Leader L. G. Maxton; Flight Lieutenant H. M. G. Parker; Flight Lieutenant A. C. Stevens; Flying Officer M. H. Clare; Flying Officer W. F. Murray; Flying Officer B. A. Frazer and Pilot Officer D. C. T. Bennett.

(W. LINIKER

Not the prettiest vessel ever to enter the Haven maybe, but the RAF's one and only Seaplane Dock served the Pembroke Dock flying-boat station well in the 1930s. Better known locally as the 'Floating Dock' — and among its crew as 'HMS Flat Iron' — this vessel was towed to Pembroke Dock early in 1932 and remained there until the time of the Munich Crisis in 1938. Weighing in at 1,000 tons gross, 400 tons nett, this unique vessel had a strong local link as it had been designed by Mr. John N. Narbeth, son of a Pembroke Dock lay preacher, and who started his illustrious career in the Admiralty as a shipwright apprentice at Pembroke Dockyard in 1877. He rose to become Assistant Director of Naval Construction, retiring in 1923. Strange it was that his floating dock should find such a role many years later at the town where he spent his early years.

The Seaplane Dock could partly submerge, allowing one or two flying-boats to be 'taken aboard'. The Dock was then raised to bring the aircraft clear of the water. In all weathers and at all times of the year, various types of aircraft were taken into the Dock for maintenance work — and engines changes, tailplane changes and even mainplane changes were regular occurrences.

During the Empire Air Days in the 1930s, 'HMS Flat Iron' was a big attraction and civilians were allowed to look over the vessel. And during regular maintenance periods in Milford Docks this unique vessel always drew large crowds of onlookers. The Seaplane Dock left Pembroke Dock in 1938 and was towed to Invergordon, Scotland.

△ The RAF Seaplane Dock with a Southampton — minus its tailplane — aboard. The vessel could take any craft with a draught of up to seven feet.

▷ 'HMS Flat Iron' viewed from astern, with a Southampton high and dry.

BOTH H. ROGERS

The skyline of Pier Road, Tremeyrick Street and Arthur Street, Pembroke Dock, is still partly familiar fifty years on. Southampton flying-boats ride on moorings in the early 1930s. In the original photograph nine Southamptons could be identified and as Pembroke Dock's complement of aircraft at the time was only four, this must have been taken when another unit was visiting — perhaps for an exercise in conjunction with the Royal Navy. Nearest aircraft is N9901, one of the first production batch of Southampton Mark 1s which had wooden hulls. Another of the Southamptons, S1038, is a Mark I while the others which can be identified — S1233 and S1421 — are Mark II 'boats with Duralumin hulls.

J. POINTER

By 1934, No 210. Squadron had expanded considerably and 56 officers and men joined the Commanding Officer, Squadron Leader A. F. Lang, MBE, for this official line-up.

K. EVANS

RAF Pembroke Dock's Marine Craft Section in 1932, an all civilian manned unit under the command of Flight Lieutenant H. A. Castaldini, a retired RAF officer. Pictured are: Back row (left to right): LAC Saville, Fred Griffiths, Jimmy Evans, Jock Sharp, Howard Hitchings, Tom Bastin, Bob Yolland. Front row (left to right): Vernon Evans, Jimmy Doney, George Russan, Flight Lieutenant H. A. Castaldini, Charlie Wetherley, Fred Morgan.

J. EVANS

Between 1931 and the beginning of the war, No. 210 Squadron operated six different types of flying-boat, among them the Short Rangoon. Powered by three Bristol Jupiter engines, the Rangoons cruised at all of 92 mph and could, at a push, top 115 mph. Only six Rangoons were built and No. 210 Squadron operated the type between August 1935, and September 1936. This photograph, whilst not taken locally, captures fully the graceful lines of this radial-engined biplane 'boat. S1433 served with No. 210 Squadron.

SHORT BROS, BELFAST

A gleaming silver giant at rest: The Singapore Mark III, of which 37 were built for the RAF, was one of the mainstays of the RAF flying-boat squadrons in the middle 1930s. Another from the famous Short stable, the Mark III was powered by four Rolls-Royce Kestrel engines in tractor and pusher pairs and its maximum speed was 145 mph. At home and abroad it served with seven RAF squadrons and was still in service in the Far East in 1941. K3592, superbly photographed by Short Bros, was the first Mark III and first flew on 15th June, 1934. It served with the Marine Aircraft Experimental Establishment at Felixstowe before going to No. 210 Squadron at Pembroke Dock. No. 210 took this and three other Singapores out to re-equip No. 205 Squadron at Seletar, Singapore, early in 1935, sadly losing one of the aircraft en route in a crash on Sicily. K3592 stayed with No. 205 Squadron, eventually being Struck Off RAF Charge in December, 1937.

SHORT BROS, BELFAST

The last in a long line of biplane flying-boats to serve at RAF Pembroke Dock — the Supermarine Stranraer. Designed by R. J. Mitchell (creator of the Spitfire) the Stranraer first flew in 1935 and was initially used by No. 228 Squadron at Pembroke Dock. This squadron reformed in December 1936, and used various types of flying-boat before becoming an all-Stranraer unit in August 1938. Early in 1939, Sunderlands began to arrive for the squadron and the elegant Stranraers were passed to other units. This photograph — originally a postcard sold at the 1939 Empire Air Day — shows K7292 at anchor with engine covers in place. In the background is one of the early Sunderlands. K7292 served with Nos. 228, 209 and 240 Squadrons and soldiered on well into the war, being finally Struck Off RAF Charge in May 1941. The Stranraer was powered by two Bristol Pegasus engines and had a maximum speed of 165 mph. It was armed with three Lewis guns in the nose, midships and tail positions and could carry a 1,000 lb bomb load for 1,000 miles.

G. CLAYTON/W. J. DAVIES

The shape of things to come — the Imperial Airways Empire flying-boat Caledonia off Pembroke Dock on 1st September, 1937. Caledonia was the second of the famous Short S23 'C' Class Empire flying-boats. Registered G-ADHM, this aircraft was built as a long-range version for the trans-Atlantic mail service and first flew in August 1936. A year later Caledonia — under the command of Commander A. S. Wilcoxson — landed in the Haven on the second day of a three-day tour of the British Isles, its sleek monoplane lines in contrast to the biplane flying-boats of the RAF nearby. As the crew were entertained in the RAF Officers' Mess, hundreds of people had a closer look at the new arrival from dozens of small craft and from a steamer which made special trips from Hobbs Point. During the evening, 1,200 gallons of fuel were loaded into Caledonia's tanks and the following morning the silver machine rose majestically from the water and winged its way along the Welsh, Devon and Cornish coasts to Plymouth and, finally, home to Hythe, Southampton. Within a matter of months Caledonia's military sister, the Sunderland, was to make its appearance in Pembrokeshire skies for the first time. Powered by four Bristol Pegasus radial engines, the S23 Empire 'boats were capable of carrying 3½ tons of mail and 24 passengers with a cruising speed of 165 mph. Range, with extra tanks, was 2,300 miles.

VIA WESTERN TELEGRAPH

No. 228 Squadron's one and only Supermarine Scapa at its moorings with a London flying-boat in the distance. K7306 was the last of 14 Scapas built for the RAF and joined No. 228 Squadron at Pembroke Dock in 1937. Tragically, this aircraft was lost in August 1938, when it dived into the sea off Felixstowe whilst engaged on an experimental flight and all the crew of five were killed. Four of them were Welsh and included airmen from Mathry, Pembrokeshire, and St. Clears, Carmarthenshire. The Scapa was powered by two Rolls-Royce Kestrel engines giving a maximum speed of 141 mph and a range of 1,100 miles.

G. PALMER COLLECTION

No. 210 Squadron's officers, NCOs and airmen pose for an official photograph in 1938 with their Commanding Officer, Wing Commander W. N. Plenderleith. There are 79 officers and men lined up, some of the men still wearing the old style high neck tunics. Wing Commander William Noble Plenderleith had a varied and distinguished career which was to be tragically cut short at the age of 39, when he collapsed and died at the RAF station in December 1938. A Royal Flying Corps veteran who was shot down and badly wounded in the Great War, he was one of the three-man crew of a Vickers Vulture amphibian which attempted a round-the-world flight in 1924. This flight ended with a crash in Burma and a replacement aircraft also crashed later.

MRS. R. THOMAS/GROUP CAPTAIN H. D. NEWMAN

Rifles at the trail, airmen from RAF Pembroke Dock march along Bush Street on a cold December day in 1938 as the funeral procession of Wing Commander W. N. Plenderleith wends its way to Llanion Cemetery. This solemn scene was to be repeated many times at Pembroke Dock during the coming war years as the men of the flying-boat base honoured their dead.

H. BUXTON

The mighty Sunderland made its first appearance at Pembroke Dock in May 1938, and thrilled the 6,000 people who attended Empire Air Day at the air station, as well as showing its paces over other local towns. Soon afterwards, Sunderlands began to arrive at Pembroke Dock and some of them were flown by No. 210 Squadron crews to Singapore, where they re-equipped No. 230 Squadron. This photograph shows one of the first of the big 'boats — perhaps even the first to come to Pembroke Dock — being towed by an RAF Pinnace. The Sunderland already has its beaching gear in place. Key men in the operation to bring a Sunderland ashore, or to re-float it, were the two men standing knee-deep in the water. Equipped with wet suits, they had to spend lengthy amounts of time in often freezing cold water strapping or unfastening the giant wheeled legs each side of the flying-boat's hull. Theirs was not an enviable task, but one which was vital to the success of what was always a tricky operation.

W. J. DAVIES

In immaculate formation, five Sunderlands of No. 210 (General Reconnaissance) Squadron fly over Tenby — or are they? Closer examination reveals that drawings of five Sunderlands have been superimposed on an oblique shot of Tenby. This spoof photograph featured on the 1938 Christmas card sent out by members of No. 210 Squadron. The Squadron had only received its first Sunderland some months earlier and would have been hard-pressed to put five aircraft in the air simultaneously at that time.

VIA CARSLEY COLLECTION

The 7,250 people who attended the Empire Air Day at the RAF station in May 1939, were witnessing the end of an era, although most were happily unaware of this at the time. Within months, Britain was at war with Germany and RAF Pembroke Dock was to play a significant part in the war from the first day to the last. But, on that May Saturday in the last months of peace, the public were at liberty to roam freely within the Dockyard base, viewing the hangars, workshops, accommodation and the aircraft. Dominating the area were the huge silver Sunderlands of Nos. 210 and 228 Squadrons, and flying-boats took part in the flying display, along with Fairey Battle light bombers and — most interesting of all — a Hawker Hurricane fighter. A Hurricane made a high speed pass over the station, returning to fly past slowly, allowing the public to view at reasonably close quarters a fighter which was to bear the brunt of the action in the Battle of Britain just over a year later. Not to be outdone by its more illustrious contemporaries, the Vickers Supermarine Walrus amphibian, pictured here, demonstrated its unique ability to taxi down the slipway into the water, take off and give a display. This particular Walrus, L2314, was with the Floatplane Training Unit at the time, but within days had been transferred to the Admiralty for service with the Royal Navy.

GROUP CAPTAIN G. A. BOLLAND

C-Charlie in both natural elements .... eager youngsters who attended the 1939 Empire Air Day at RAF Pembroke Dock quickly snapped up the postcards depicting RAF aircraft. One showed Sunderland Mark I L2163 in flying pose. This aircraft was one of the first allocated to No. 210 Squadron and is seen in pre-war silver finish complete with squadron badge and individual letter below the cockpit. L2163 had a lengthy RAF career and finally was lost in January, 1942, when it sank in a gale at Stranraer whilst on charge with No. 228 Squadron.

G. CLAYTON

C-Charlie at a mooring off Pembroke Dock, with Neyland in the background. This pre-war photograph was snapped by Roy Hordley, a keen amateur photographer.

R. HORDLEY

First casualty: RAF Pembroke Dock's first wartime loss occurred just seven days after the outbreak of war on 3rd September, 1939, but happily there were no injuries to the crew. No. 228 Squadron — one of the two resident RAF squadrons — had been detached to Alexandria and Malta since mid-1939, only to be recalled soon after the declaration of war. N6135, still carrying its pre-war code letters BH-U, returned on 10th September and on approaching the Pembrokeshire coast encountered bad weather with low cloud. There was a heavy swell on the water and when landing downwind at Angle Bay, the Sunderland's floats were damaged. Later, the damaged flying-boat was towed up river and near the RAF Station it turned turtle and sank. Several days later the Sunderland was salvaged and pulled up on the shore off Front Street, close to one of the Victorian gun forts. Too badly damaged to be repaired, N6135 was scrapped on site — a loss the RAF could ill afford at any time, especially at such a critical stage in the war when they had so few flying boats.

D. PURCELL

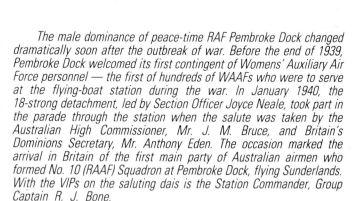

The male dominance of peace-time RAF Pembroke Dock changed dramatically soon after the outbreak of war. Before the end of 1939, Pembroke Dock welcomed its first contingent of Womens' Auxiliary Air Force personnel — the first of hundreds of WAAFs who were to serve at the flying-boat station during the war. In January 1940, the 18-strong detachment, led by Section Officer Joyce Neale, took part in the parade through the station when the salute was taken by the Australian High Commissioner, Mr. J. M. Bruce, and Britain's Dominions Secretary, Mr. Anthony Eden. The occasion marked the arrival in Britain of the first main party of Australian airmen who formed No. 10 (RAAF) Squadron at Pembroke Dock, flying Sunderlands. With the VIPs on the saluting dais is the Station Commander, Group Captain R. J. Bone.

MRS. J. SKELTON

That timeless favourite, 'Cinderella', was the choice for the RAF's Pantomime staged at the County School Hall, Pembroke Dock, on 8th January, 1941. Running to no less than nine scenes, the panto featured a main cast of 11 with a WAAF chorus, a male quartet and the station orchestra, and the proceeds were in aid of HM Forces Welfare Club, Pembroke Dock. The cast list was: Prince Charming — ASO Tanner; Cinderella — Cpl. Phillips; Buttons — A/C Yates; Araminta — F/Lieut Gray; Delphinia — F/Lieut Clarke; Baron Hardup — F/O Anderson; Fairy Godmother — SO Neale; Friar — W/O Coslett; Villager — Cpl. Hibbert; Gipsy — A/C Bond; Page — ACW Penrhyn Jones. The WAAF Chorus was made up of ACWs Aikman, Thomas, Lee, Shelley, Fisher and Rees and the members of the male quartet were S/Ldr Robinson, ACs Crocker, Smith and Pearce. The solo pianist was Cpl. Mival.

MRS. J. SKELTON

Flying Dutchmen ... among the most unusual aircraft to operate out of Pembroke Dock were the Fokker T-VIII-W floatplanes, flown by Dutch crews. With the German invasion of the Netherlands, several of these modern twin-engined floatplanes were flown to Britain and came to Pembroke Dock to form up as No. 320 Squadron, Royal Air Force. Their stay at PD was brief, as shortage of spares and the loss of two aircraft on operations forced the Fokkers to be withdrawn and No. 320 Squadron converted on to Avro Ansons in a landplane role. As RAF aircraft the Fokkers carried standard British roundels but retained the Dutch national marking — an inverted orange triangle, edged in black, — on the nose.

△ These photographs show a Fokker airborne over Milford Haven, and one of the floatplanes at Pembroke Dock on the 'sledge' — a moveable platform fitted into one of the old Dockyard slipways and used early in the war to bring floatplanes ashore. Just behind the Dutch aircraft is a Swordfish floatplane with wings folded. This was operated by a Royal Navy training squadron, also 'in residence' at Pembroke Dock at the time.

ROYAL NETHERLANDS NAVAL HISTORICAL DEPARTMENT

△ A purposeful looking Catalina of No. 210 Squadron on patrol, four bombs slung under its wings. Just discernible on the original print were the code letters 'DA' for No. 210 Squadron and the serial number, AH569. The Catalina was the other mainstay of Coastal Command's flying-boat squadrons and served with the RAF from 1941 until the end of the war with Japan (one even operated with the RAF before the war). Although slower than its bigger contemporary, the Sunderland, the twin-engined Catalina had a prodigious endurance and stayed aloft for over 24 hours on occasions. With a maximum speed of 190 knots it had a range of 4,000 miles, something like 1,000 miles more than the later marks of Sunderland. At Pembroke Dock Catalinas served mainly with Nos. 209 and 210 Squadrons in the mid-war years. This particular aircraft was photographed from a No. 209 Squadron 'Cat' off Scotland and it poses a query for historians. Officially, AH569 is not listed as serving with No. 210 Squadron, yet it has the squadron code letters and the serial was readable. Its official history is that it served with Nos. 413 and 209 Squadrons and was Struck Off Charge as spares in December 1941. Bombs carried by flying-boats early in the war did not prove to be very effective against German submarines and it was not until the naval Torpex-filled depth charge was modified for dropping from the air, that the 'Cats' and the Sunderlands were given real 'teeth' against the U-Boats.

L. J. B. WRIGHT

A Sunderland's view of the RAF Station and local area, 2nd May, 1943. So well camouflaged are the two large hangars — painted to represent rows of houses — that they merge well into their surroundings. The white-hulled Sunderlands, in contrast, stand out prominently. The shadow of the photographing Sunderland can be seen on the Royal Naval hospital in the foreground.

GROUP CAPTAIN G. A. BOLLAND

The Marine Craft Section were the winners of the RAF Pembroke Dock Inter-Section Sports Championship for the season 1942-43. Here, the winning team lines up for a victory photograph outside the MCS Headquarters.

H. THRELFALL

▷ *Where many a dramatic story was unfolded ... the Intelligence Room at Pembroke Dock in 1944. On the right is a 'Landmarks and Landfalls' relief of the Western Approaches, illustrated with many photographs of what flying-boat crews would see from the air. Models of many types of Allied and Axis aircraft fly from the ceiling, while a poster on the door depicts a British 'tin hat' with the age-old warning: "Keep it under your hat!"*

M. N. ANDERSON

△ *The RAF Sick Quarters at Pembroke Dock, 1945, with Flight Sergeant Williamston standing in the doorway. An RAF medical van awaits the call to action in front of one of the familiar Georgian buildings, which were, and still are, a feature of the old Dockyard base.*

DR. D. B. STEWART

▷ *Officers of No. 119 Sunderland Squadron pictured in late 1942 or early 1943. At the time the Commanding Officer (fifth from left, front row) was Wing Commander D. McC. Gordon, AFC.*

S. SAIT

PD around the time of D-Day, June 1944. In the original photograph, 25 flying-boats could be counted — either 'on the hard' within the RAF Station or on moorings and all but one of them Sunderlands. The lone Catalina is on the mooring on the extreme right. Four of the big 'boats were moored downstream of Neyland and Llanstadwell, while further down the Haven various vessels could be seen off Milford Haven town, either trawlers or ships of a convoy.

M. N. ANDERSON

Royal visitor ... in the shadow of Sunderlands, His Royal Highness the Duke of Gloucester meets NCOs in one of Pembroke Dock's hangars in 1944. The shoulder flashes of many of the men read 'Australia' — these NCOs were attached to No. 461 Royal Australian Air Force Squadron based at Pembroke Dock.

GROUP CAPTAIN G. A. BOLLAND

▷ 'On the Step' . . . a beautiful picture of a beautiful white bird. Sunderland P-Peter, NJ 176, Pegasus engines at full power, snapped just before take-off. At one stage of the war Coastal Command dispensed with codes for its aircraft and allocated individual numbers to the Squadrons at its various bases. NJ176 served with No. 422 (RCAF) Squadron during the war and was photographed at Castle Archdale, Northern Ireland, the squadron's other wartime base. This Sunderland had a lengthy post-war career. After conversion to Mark V standard it served with No. 88 Squadron and was written off in November, 1949, when it crashed on take-off at Seletar, Singapore.

C. ROBLIN

△ Almost home is S-Sugar, one of No. 201 Squadron's Sunderlands. This photograph was taken sometime in 1944, by which time No. 201 had adopted 'NS' as its squadron codes.

M. N. ANDERSON

◁ Just one of the many Sunderlands which graced the Milford Haven Waterway during the war years. DV980, a Short Bros. built Mark III, probably pictured on one of the moorings located between Neyland and Milford Haven on the north shore of the Haven. A weather-beaten and war-weary veteran, DV980 served with Nos. 246, 228 and 423 (Canadian) Squadrons, finally ending its days in a training role with No. 131 Operational Training Unit, Northern Ireland. This aircraft was Struck Off RAF Charge in June 1945 and when pictured was probably with No. 228 Squadron.

M. N. ANDERSON

They're under starter's orders ... but dice, rather than fillies, were the runners in this horse race game played by Australian and RAF personnel at Llanion Barracks.

W. DANN

The Empire marches ... Australians and New Zealanders proudly march through the RAF station during one of the ANZAC Day parades. The buildings look distinctly war-scarred.

W. DANN

Flying-boat history was made on 29th May, 1943, when Sunderland Mark II, T9114, made a successful landing at Angle aerodrome, the RAF station a few miles to the west of Pembroke Dock. At the controls was Flying Officer Gordon Singleton of No. 461 Squadron, Royal Australian Air Force. Earlier, Singleton and his crew had made a daring air-sea rescue in the Atlantic when they had landed on the open sea to pick up survivors of a ditched Sunderland. Hours later, after transferring the survivors and some of his crew to a French destroyer (which had also towed the Sunderland in very heavy seas), the flying-boat skipper was faced with either scuttling his aircraft or attempting to take off. Choosing to try and get airborne, Singleton and his skeleton crew heaved sighs of relief as the Sunderland at last lifted off the water, only to discover that a huge hole had been smashed in the hull. A landing on water was out of the question, so the Australian signalled Pembroke Dock that he was to attempt a landing on Angle aerodrome - something never before tried with a 27-ton flying-boat. In a masterful landing Singleton brought T9114 down on the grass parallel with the runway. The hull cut a giant furrow in the earth, the Sunderland titled over onto its port side, the float crumpled and the historic landing was over. T9114 never flew again, despite the valiant efforts made to recover it from the aerodrome. Put back on its beaching gear, the Sunderland was towed to West Angle Bay -after several hedges had been removed. As Mark II Sunderland were obsolescent the decision was made to scrap the aircraft, and this was carried out at West Angle Bay. Today a plaque on the car park -commemorating RAF Angle - also recalls this unique flying-boat landing.

AUSTRALIAN WAR MEMORIAL

'Blitzville' — that was the name given to PD by the men of the American Navy Catalina squadron which spent several months at the station in 1943. Patrol Squadron Sixty-Three (VP-63), the first US Navy squadron to fly out of the UK, was known as the 'Mad Cats' on account of the Magnetic Anomaly Detection equipment carried. The squadron flew Bay of Biscay patrols, along with the RAF Sunderlands, and lost one Catalina in operations out of PD between July and late December 1943, before moving to North Africa. While at Pembroke Dock VP-63 had a change of command ceremony with Commander E. O. Wagner handing over to Lieutenant Commander Curtis H. Hutchings. The photograph shows Lieutenant Commander Hutchings inspecting some of his men. In the background is a Sunderland.

REAR ADMIRAL C. H. HUTCHINGS, USN

The Americans called them PBYs, the British called them Catalinas, and what fine machines they were. An American Navy PBY-5, similar to the ones operated by VP-63 out of Pembroke Dock in 1943.

US NAVY

Just how many people can you get on, in and under a Sunderland? No. 461 Squadron, RAAF, tried their best towards the end of the war and around 100 men clambered onto the wings of an obliging Sunderland, plus wedging themselves into the nose turret well. Underneath the officers lined up for a more formal photograph.

W. DANN

A remarkable photograph showing the first — and perhaps only — time when a Sunderland was taxied ashore under its own power. This was an experiment to see whether time could be saved by fitting the beaching gear at the moorings and then taxiing the aircraft up the slipway. The experiment was successful, but it demanded a very experienced pilot, otherwise the beaching gear and the aircraft would be damaged. The pilot for this experiment — in March 1943 — was the commanding officer of No. 308 Ferry Training Unit at Pembroke Dock, Flight Lieutenant Derek Martin.

WING COMMANDER D. MARTIN

△ Here's to Victory! Hats and beer glasses are raised in yet another toast as just a few of PD's personnel celebrate VE-Day in the Sergeant's Mess.

B. J. LYONS

▷ A section of the Dockyard wall shows the marks of war as the WAAF band march along Fort Road, led by Drum Major LAC Phillips.

B. J. LYONS

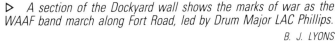

△ The Mayor of Pembroke, Alderman W. J. J. Phillips, of Gwyther Street, and Air Marshal G. O. Johnson take the salute at Albion Square, Pembroke Dock, as members of No. 422 Squadron, RCAF, march past on their third anniversary parade. Air Marshal Johnson, the Air Officer Commander in Chief, Royal Canadian Air Force Overseas, was the reviewing officer for the parade. Behind him is Group Captain W. H. Hutton, Officer Commanding, RAF Pembroke Dock, and Squadron Officer Henderson, of the RCAF Women's Division.

DR. D. B. STEWART

◁ Canadians on parade: Led by the newly-formed bugle and pipe band, men of No. 422 Squadron, Royal Canadian Air Force, proudly march up Water Street on their way from Llanion Barracks to the RAF station. The date was 24th May, 1945, and the occasion was the third anniversary of the founding of No. 422 Squadron, which had been based at Pembroke Dock since November 1944. Water Street, 40 years and more on, still looks very much the same as on that May day just after the European war had ended.

DR. D. B. STEWART

The old and the new . . . Sunderland V SZ575 of No. 230 Squadron leads a unique Coastal Command flypast over Pembroke Dock in May 1955. On the left is the American-built Neptune which served with four RAF squadrons between 1952 and 1956, whilst on the right is the British-built Avro Shackleton, which was eventually to completely supersede the Sunderland in RAF service. SZ575 was one of the longest serving Sunderlands, operating with both Nos. 230 and 201 Squadrons at PD. It was finally Struck Off Charge in October 1957, after the squadrons had disbanded.

WING COMMANDER A. M. G. LYWOOD

Squadron Leader R. A. N. McCready, officers and aircrew of No 201 Squadron pictured at Pembroke Dock, c1953. In the background is Sunderland V VB889, the last Sunderland to be built by Blackburns. This Sunderland was Struck Off RAF Charge in August, 1956, and sold for scrap a year later.

(MASTER NAVIGATOR G. KELLY

Odd one out among PD's post-war Sunderlands was the Station's Sea Otter amphibian. A number of Sea Otters — successors to the famous Walrus — were used at the RAF station in the late 1940s and early 1950s, although there was only one here at a time. This Sea Otter is believed to be JN135. It is being towed as a refueller approaches.

G. TYLER

The well populated 'Wet Dock', c 1950. In residence are (from left): a ferry boat, bomb scow, two seaplane tenders (Nos. 437 and 440) and a refueller.

G. TYLER

A long way from PD . . . Sunderland V SZ567 of No. 230 Squadron against the chilling background of Greenland's icy wastes. Between 1951 and 1954 the Pembroke Dock squadrons were involved in flying support missions for the British North Greenland Expedition. During the short Arctic summers, the Sunderlands were used to airlift stores from Young Sound — on Greenland's north-eastern side — to Britannia Lake, 190 miles inland. In 1954, No. 230 Squadron's aircraft flew again to Britannia Lake to pick up the Expedition team, equipment and 12 Husky dogs! The four Sunderlands brought their charges back to Pembroke Dock in August, and the photograph of their triumphant return features on the cover of this book. SZ567, subject of this fine shot, was Struck Off Charge in October 1957.

P. RANDALL

△ Royal escort . . . three Pembroke Dock Sunderlands flew as escort in May 1954, to the Royal Yacht Britannia which brought the Queen and her family home from an overseas tour. This photograph — taken from D-Dog of No. 201 Squadron (piloted by Flying Officer 'Shorty' Bartrum) — shows M-Mother, RN304, of the Flying-Boat Training Squadron (piloted by Wing Commander J. W. Louw, OBE, DFC, Officer Commanding Flying Wing), and Z-Zebra of No. 230 Squadron (commanded by Flight Lieutenant Stan Bowater, DFC) over the Royal Yacht. For the record, RN304 served on until the end of Pembroke Dock's flying-boat days, being Struck Off Charge in September 1957.

B. LUCAS/J. POINTER

◁ During the Queen's first visit as reigning monarch to Pembrokeshire, in August 1955, she used the RAF pier at Pembroke Dock as an embarkation and disembarkation point. Here, she is pictured with Air Vice-Marshal G. W. Tuttle, CB, OBE, DFC, Air Officer Commanding No. 19 Group, Coastal Command. Following is Group Captain P. A. Lombard, DFC, the last Station Commander at RAF Pembroke Dock.

△ Crewmen line the wings of a No. 230 Squadron Sunderland as the Royal Barge, White Ensign flying, moves down the Haven towards the Royal Yacht Britannia. Hundreds of people line the bank and the slipways on the Neyland side.

PHOTOS: SQUADRON LEADER A. NICOLL

▽ RAF Pembroke Dock's memorable way of saying farewell to HM The Queen in August 1955. Eight Sunderlands of Nos. 201 and 230 Squadrons and the Flying-Boat Training Squadron made up this unique formation which was snapped over the rooftops.

I. E. MORGAN

Pilots of No. 201 Squadron drew lots to select who would be the lucky one to fly the last RAF Sunderland to land on the Thames. The occasion was Battle of Britain Week, 1956, and the lucky pilot was Flight Lieutenant Alan Nicoll. Here, his aircraft, the long-serving DP198, rests at anchor by Tower Bridge — the Tower of London a splendid backdrop.

SQUADRON LEADER A. NICOLL

Almost the end of an era, as officers and men of No. 230 Squadron pose for a last official photograph before the squadron disbanded in February 1957. At the time, the Commanding Officer was Squadron Leader P. G. Adams, DSO. Behind the group is Sunderland DP198, one of the longest-serving of an illustrious breed. Built at Short's factory on Lake Windermere, DP198 saw wartime service with No. 423 (RCAF) Squadron before being converted to Mark V standard, subsequently serving with Nos. 209, 205 and 201 Squadrons. After the two resident squadrons disbanded at Pembroke Dock, DP198 was flown out to RAF Seletar, Singapore, to serve again with No. 205 Squadron, the last RAF unit to operate the most famous of all the flying-boats. No. 205 Squadron completely converted to Shackletons in May 1959, and the honour fell to DP198 to make the last Sunderland flight in RAF service. The end was not long in coming for DP198 and its contemporaries after this historic flight. Stripped of engines and other useful equipment, the Far East Sunderlands were unceremoniously discarded, ending their days in a Singapore scrapyard. Officially, DP198 was Struck Off RAF Charge on 1st June, 1959, one of the last of the many.

D. W. WALLACE